DINAH ZIKE'S

NOTEBOOK FOLDABLES®
Linear Measurement
Facts, Operations, and Properties

Dinah Zike, M.Ed.

⊲ **W9-CNU-594**

Copyright © 2011, Dinah Zike
Dinah-Might Adventures, LP
San Antonio, Texas
www.dinah.com

Important Hints for Using This Book:

This is not a scope and sequence book. Pick and choose the grade level-appropriate Notebook Foldables® you need to help students master the concepts of linear measurement. Glue the anchor tabs of these dependent Foldables into spiral notebooks, composition books, or large Foldable projects.

- Main ideas, questions, titles, examples, and equations are found on the front of the tabs.
- Student responses are written on the back of and under the tabs.
- Student responses might include the following: definitions, examples, related problems, word problems, related facts, and more.

Help students relate the factual information on the front of the tabs to concrete, memorable math experiences.

Note that the center spread contains a removable acetate sheet of small transparent rulers that are to be cut out for student use. One side contains six customary six-inch rulers, and the other side contains rulers in metric units. These are intended to serve as complementary tools to the Notebook Foldables templates.

How to Use Any Paper, Including Lined Paper or Templates, to Make Notebook Foldables®:

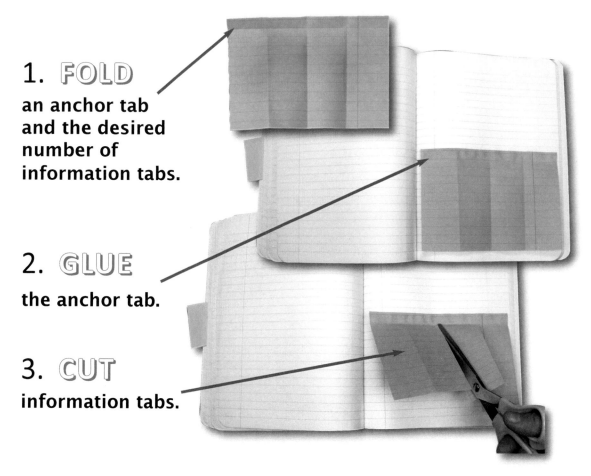

1. FOLD
an anchor tab and the desired number of information tabs.

2. GLUE
the anchor tab.

3. CUT
information tabs.

Linear Measurement
Facts, Operations, and Properties

Welcome! Many of you have been using my Foldables (originally called 3-D interactive graphic organizers) since the 1970s, and you have converted, or are in the process of converting, to Notebook Foldables. Through the years, notebooking in many forms has proven effective for generating, collecting, and organizing activities for instruction, practice, and assessment. Notebooking also provides a venue for recording student observations, questions, and opinions while immersing students in academic vocabulary.

Notebook Foldables can be integrated easily into any notebooking program. For more in-depth information on Notebook Foldables strategies, you might view my Notebook Foldables® book and CD, which won a 2011 Teachers' Choice Award.

This series of Notebooking Central booklets is a response to teachers who asked for Notebook Foldables that:
- provide graphics to aid comprehension and memory
- provide duplicable front tabs that generate student responses on the back of tabs, underneath tabs, and on the notebook page surrounding tabs
- provide ideas for the use of Notebook Foldables within different content areas

Linear Measurement is an area of mathematics that poses difficulties for many students. No matter how many strategies for measurement a teacher has in his/her arsenal of teaching aids, some students will still need "something different" to help them master the basics. This booklet involves a focus on linear measurement, including customary and metric units.

I taught Remedial Math 1st-6th for several years in the 1980s. My goal was to develop a variety of visual and kinesthetic aids to teach basic facts, and to present facts and concepts in different sequences, until I could determine what worked best for individual students. I have continued to use and redefine these aids over the last thirty years, and I'm happy to share some of them with you in this duplicable format. As you flip through the book you will see that I've also included Notebook Foldables® activities that are designed specifically to be used in spirals, composition books, or large Foldable projects.

When using Notebooking Central booklets, duplicate the pages you consider the most important, and use suggestions from other pages to generate your own ideas. Present a concept, then have students outline and design their own Notebook Foldables.

Please join our free e-group so we can keep you posted on new books in this series. We will never share or sell our e-group list. We hope to see you in the near future, either at conferences or at the Dinah Zike Academy. Best wishes!

Dinah Zike

Table of Contents

What Can Be Measured?

Describe

What can be measured?

Describe

What can be measured?

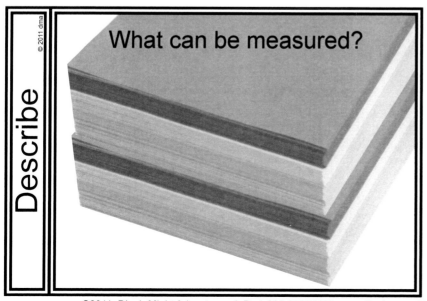

Describe

What can be measured?

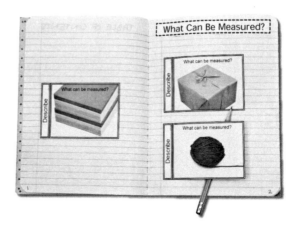

Compare Measures

more of • less of • taller • shorter • longer • wider • narrower

© 2011 dma

ream of copy paper

ream of notebook paper

more of • less of • taller • shorter • longer • wider • narrower

© 2011 dma

ream of copy paper

ream of notebook paper

Inch, Foot, Yard

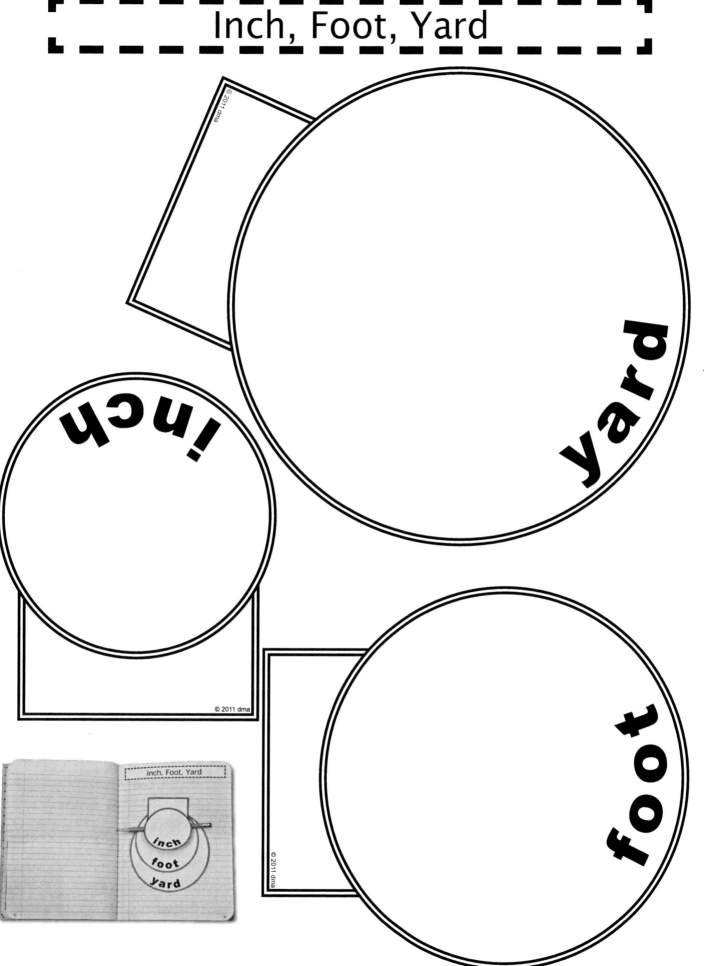

inch

yard

foot

Linear Measurement: Understand the relationships between different standard units of measurement.

© 2011 dma

© 2011 dma

Inch, Foot, Yard

inch
foot
yard

3

Linear Measurement: Conversions, equivalencies, and relationships. Express measurements in terms of larger and smaller units.

Units of Conversion

inch			
foot	12 inches		
yard	36 inches	3 feet	
mile	63,360 inches	5,280 feet	1,760 yards

Record measurement equivalents for feet and inches. Use for reference.

feet	inches	number pair
1 foot	12 inches	(1, 12)
2 feet		
3 feet		
4 feet		
5 feet		
6 feet		

VKVs: Standard Abbreviations

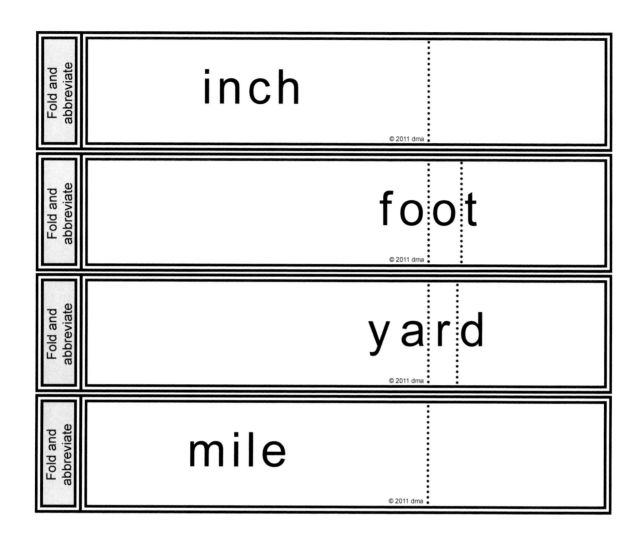

Fold and abbreviate — inch
© 2011 dma

Fold and abbreviate — foot
© 2011 dma

Fold and abbreviate — yard
© 2011 dma

Fold and abbreviate — mile
© 2011 dma

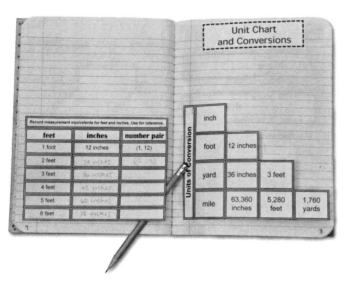

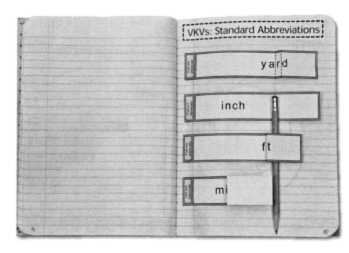

Millimeter, Centimeter, Meter

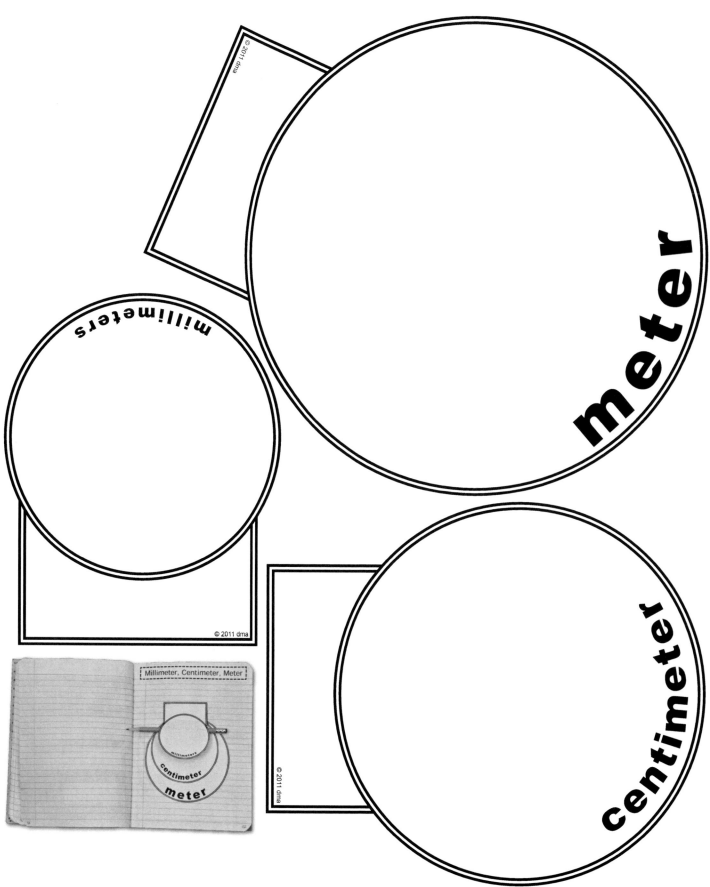

Linear Measurement: Understand the relationship between different standard units of measurement.

meter

centimeter

Millimeters

© 2011 dma

© 2011 dma

Unit Chart and Conversions

Metric Units of Conversion

millimeter			
centimeter	10 millimeters		
meter	1,000 millimeters	100 centimeters	
kilometer	1,000,000 millimeters	10,000 centimeters	1,000 meters

Record measurement equivalents for centimeter, meters, and kilometers. Use for reference.

© 2011 dma

centimeters	meters	kilometers
100	1	.001
100,000	1000	1
		2
		3
		4
		5

Linear Measurement: Understand the relationship between different standard units of measurement.

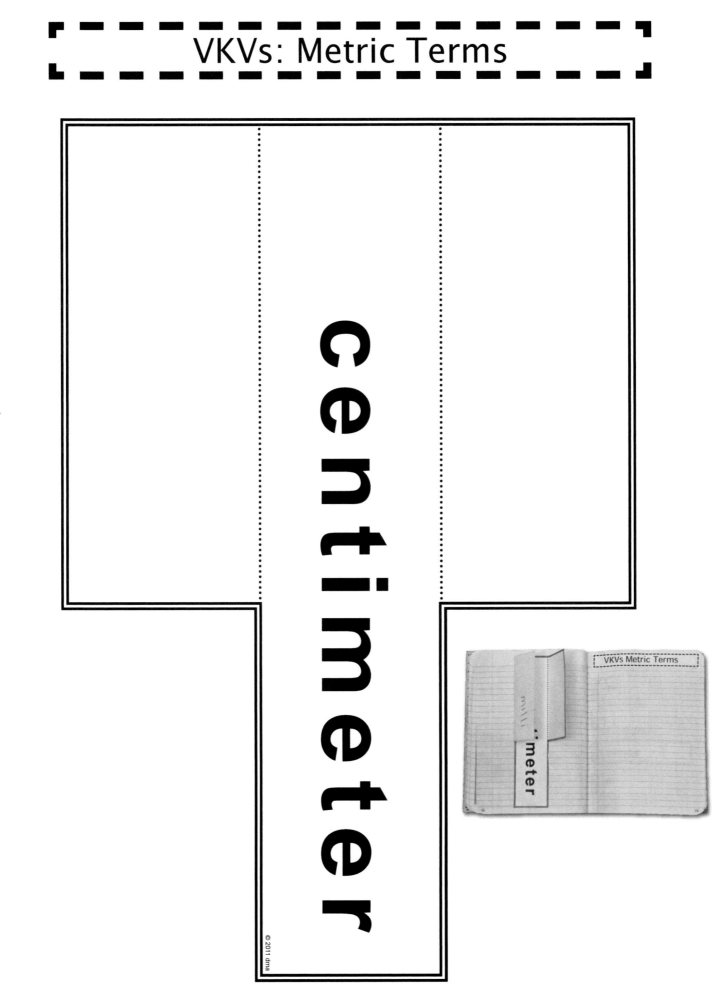

centimeter

© 2011 dma

VKVs Metric Terms

milli

meter

VKVs: Metric Abbreviations

Fold and abbreviate	millimeter

© 2011 dma

Fold and abbreviate	centimeter

© 2011 dma

Fold and abbreviate	meter

© 2011 dma

Fold and abbreviate	kilometer

© 2011 dma

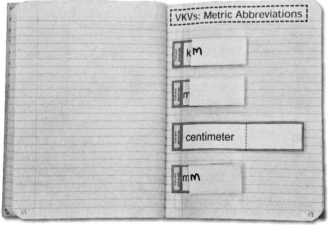

- **km (fold to cover everything except k)**
- **meter (fold over to allow m to show)**
- **cm (fold over to cover everything except c)**
- **millimeter (fold over to cover everything except m)**

Tools to Measure Length

Linear Measurement: Measure the length of an object by selecting and using appropriate tools. Understand the purpose of tools.

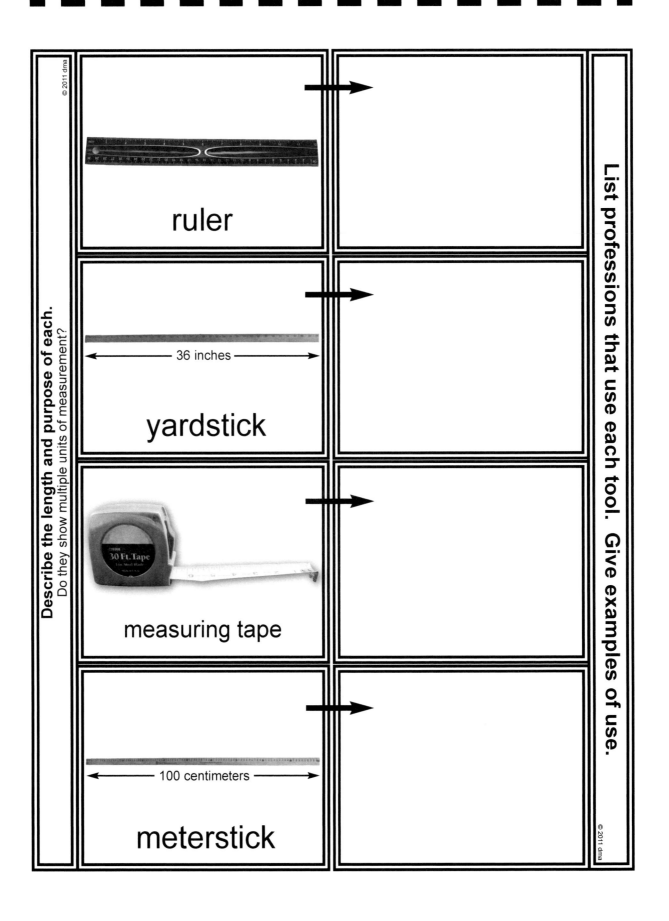

© 2011 dma

Describe the length and purpose of each.
Do they show multiple units of measurement?

ruler

←——— 36 inches ———→

yardstick

30 Ft. Tape

measuring tape

←——— 100 centimeters ———→

meterstick

List professions that use each tool. Give examples of use.

© 2011 dma

Measurable Attributes

Linear Measurement

What units would *you* use to measure each?

highway

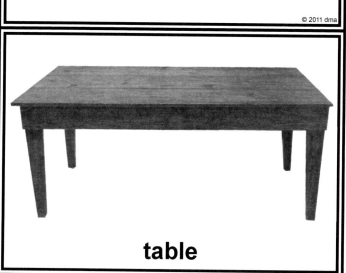

table

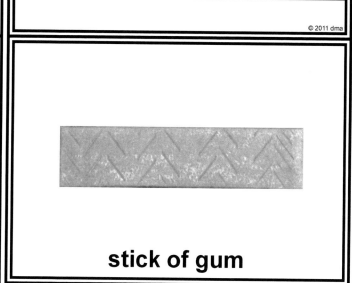

stick of gum

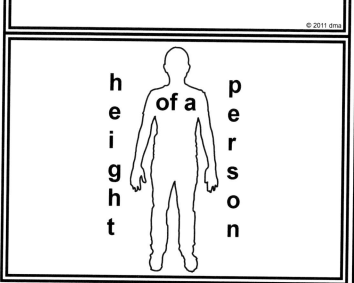

height of a person

lumber

Use Two Different Units

Linear Measurement: Measure the length of an object twice using different units of measurement.

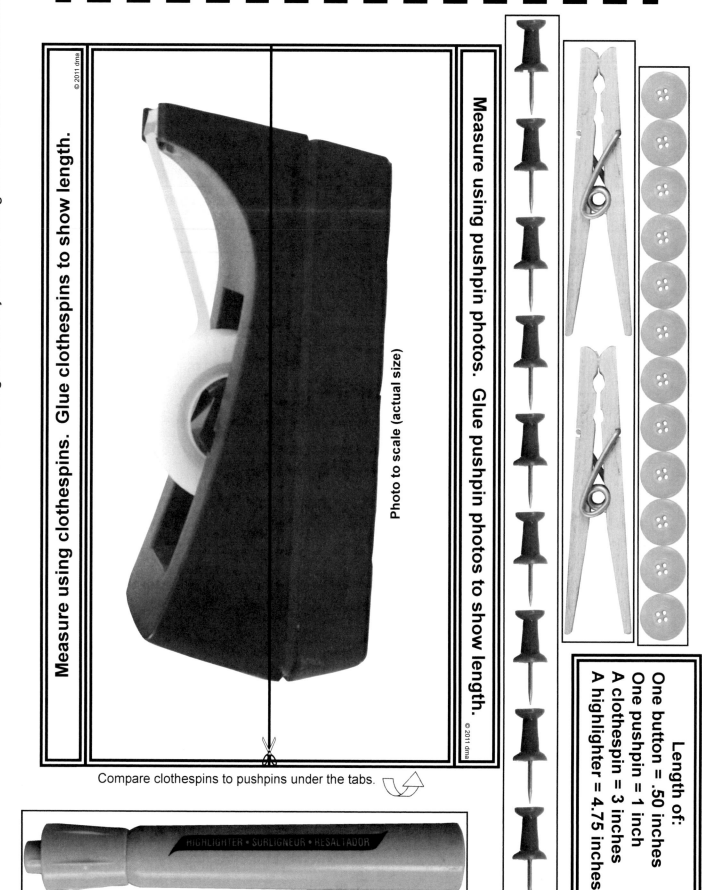

Measure using clothespins. Glue clothespins to show length.

© 2011 dma

Photo to scale (actual size)

Compare clothespins to pushpins under the tabs.

Measure using pushpin photos. Glue pushpin photos to show length.

© 2011 dma

HIGHLIGHTER • SURLIGNEUR • RESALTADOR

Length of:
One button = .50 inches
One pushpin = 1 inch
A clothespin = 3 inches
A highlighter = 4.75 inches

Use Two Different Units

Measure using a customary ruler.

Measure using a metric ruler.

© 2011 dma

© 2011 dma

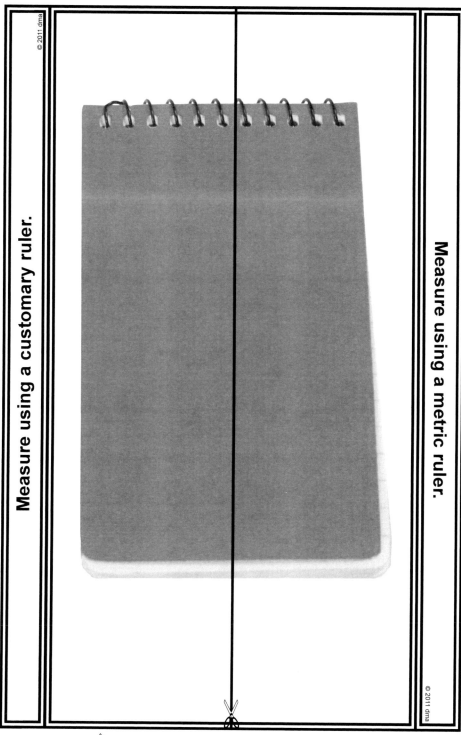

Compare measurements under the tabs.

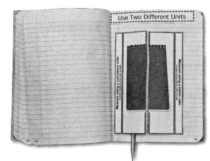

Measure With Length Units

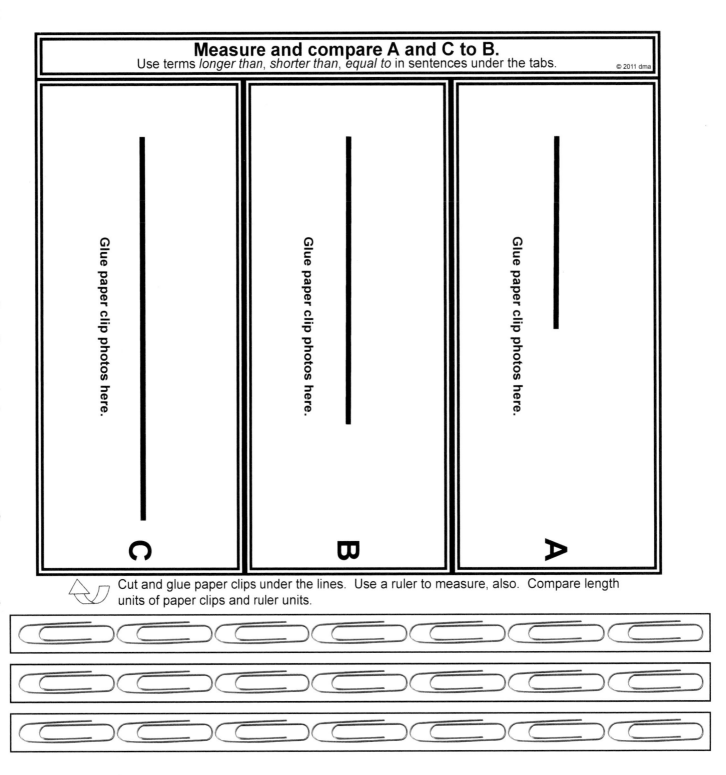

Linear Measurement: Compare the lengths of three objects using length units end to end. Use a ruler when appropriate.

Measure and compare A and C to B.
Use terms *longer than*, *shorter than*, *equal to* in sentences under the tabs.

© 2011 dma

Glue paper clip photos here.

Glue paper clip photos here.

Glue paper clip photos here.

C

B

A

Cut and glue paper clips under the lines. Use a ruler to measure, also. Compare length units of paper clips and ruler units.

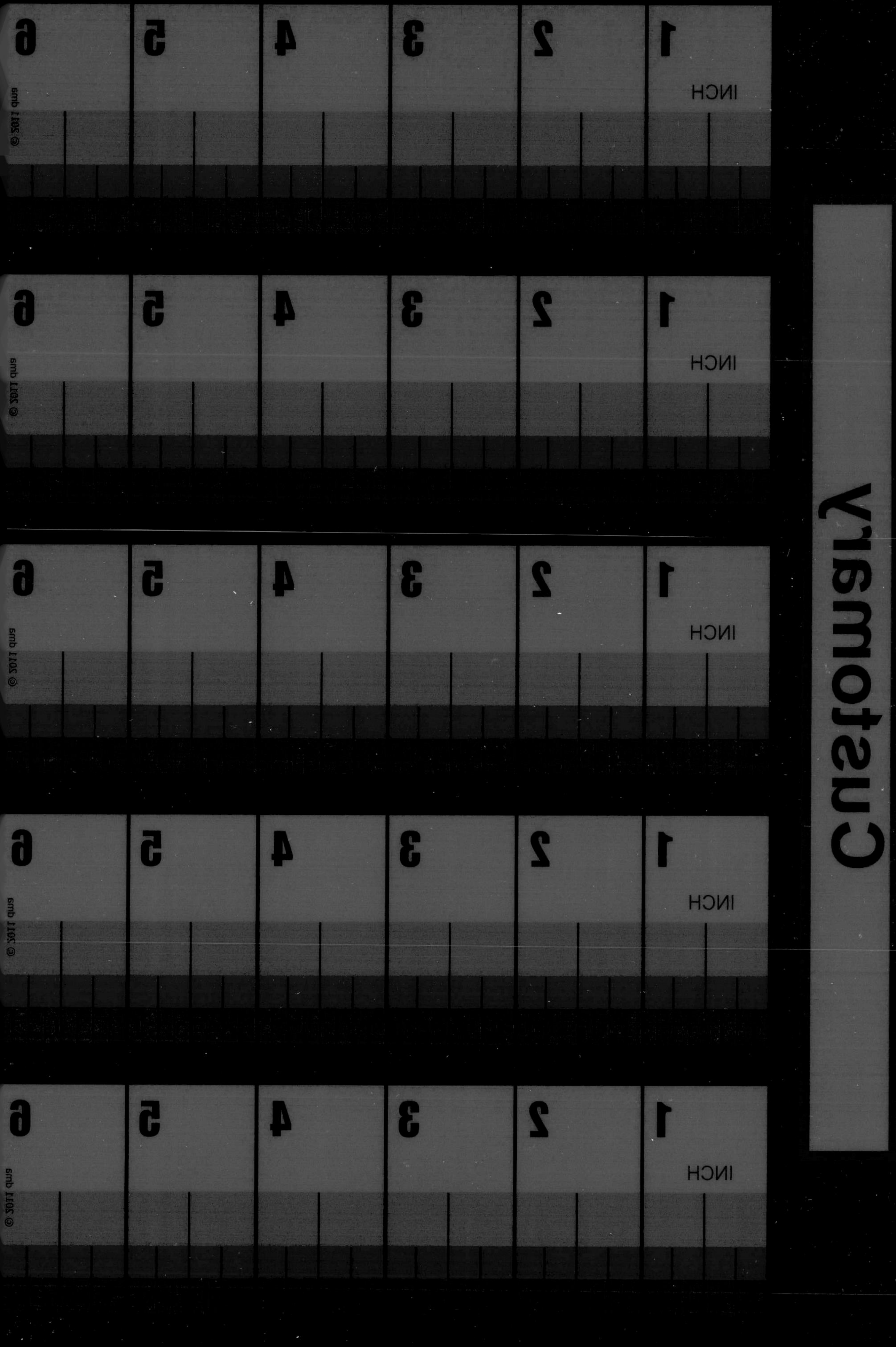

Customary

INCH
1 2 3 4 5 6
© 2011 dms

INCH
1 2 3 4 5 6
© 2011 dms

INCH
1 2 3 4 5 6
© 2011 dms

INCH
1 2 3 4 5 6
© 2011 dms

INCH
1 2 3 4 5 6
© 2011 dms

Customary

INCH 1 2 3 4 5 6

© 2011 dma

INCH 1 2 3 4 5 6

© 2011 dma

INCH 1 2 3 4 5 6

© 2011 dma

INCH 1 2 3 4 5 6

© 2011 dma

INCH 1 2 3 4 5 6

© 2011 dma

Estimate Lengths: Inches

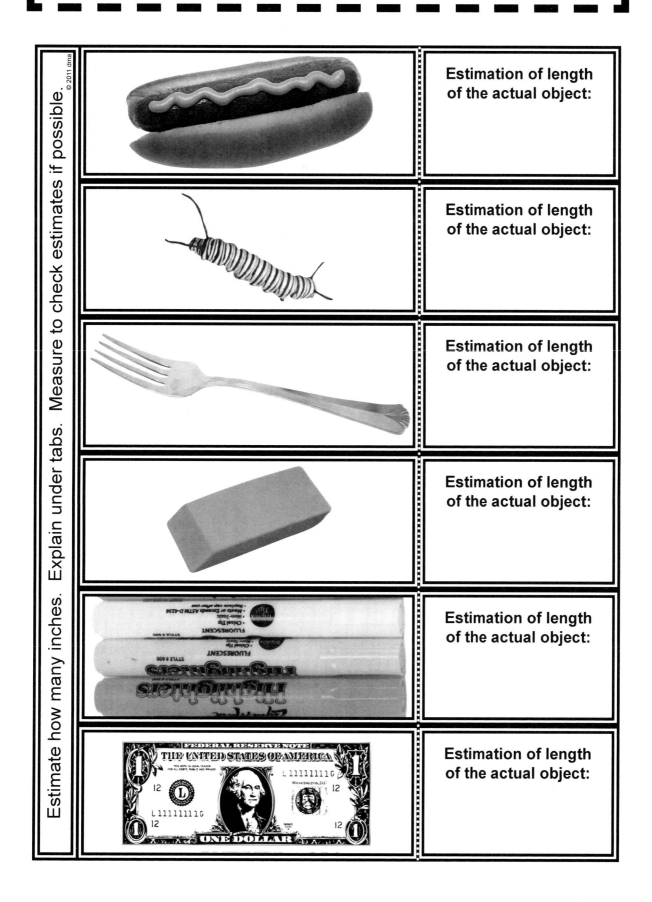

© 2011 dma

Estimate how many inches. Explain under tabs. Measure to check estimates if possible.

Estimation of length of the actual object:

Estimation of length of the actual object:

Estimation of length of the actual object:

Estimation of length of the actual object:

Estimation of length of the actual object:

Estimation of length of the actual object:

Linear Measurement: Estimate lengths using units of inches, feet, centimeters, and meters.

Estimate how many centimeters. Explain your answer under tabs.

© 2011 dma

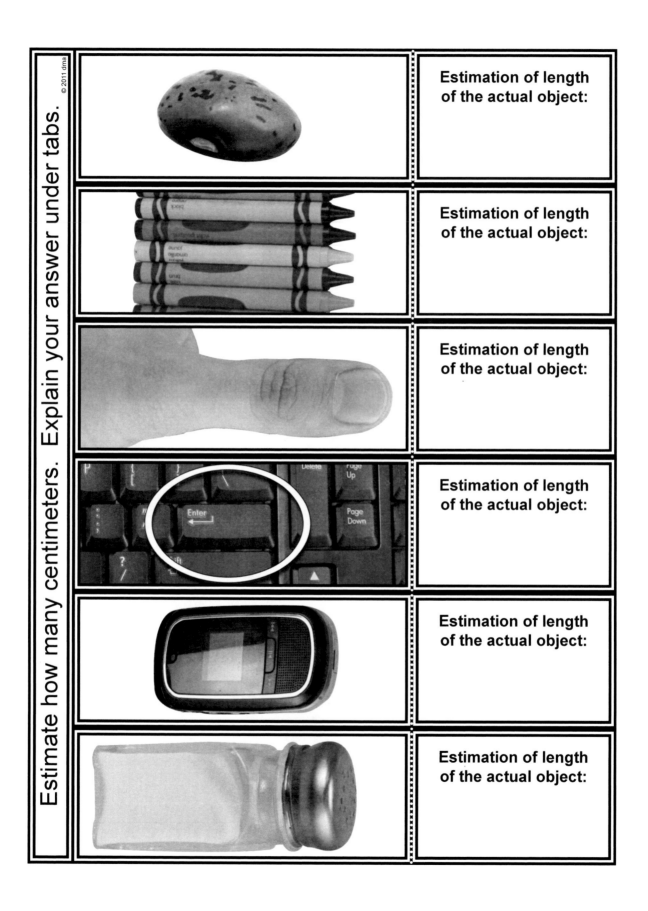

Estimation of length of the actual object:

Estimation of length of the actual object:

Estimation of length of the actual object:

Estimation of length of the actual object:

Estimation of length of the actual object:

Estimation of length of the actual object:

Estimate: Yards and Feet

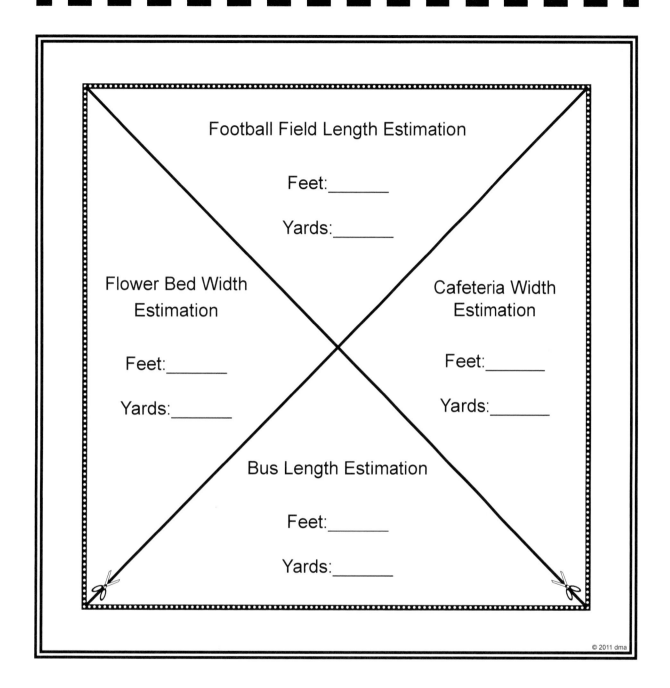

Football Field Length Estimation

Feet:_____

Yards:_____

Flower Bed Width Estimation

Feet:_____

Yards:_____

Cafeteria Width Estimation

Feet:_____

Yards:_____

Bus Length Estimation

Feet:_____

Yards:_____

© 2011 dma

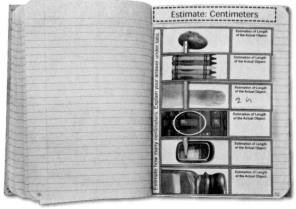

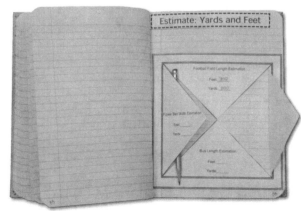

17

Measurement

- **Teachers can give students Fun math Facts for linear measurement or have students find their own Fun Facts.**

Example: The average depth of the Pacific Ocean is 15,215 feet.

Fun Fact #2

Measurement
Estimating, comparing, converting, and writing word problems with Fun Facts

Fun Fact #1

Estimating, comparing, converting, and writing word problems with Fun Facts

© 2011 dma

Measurement

© 2011 dma

Fun Fact #4

Fun Fact #3

Linear Measurement: Convert like measurement units within a given measurement system.

Inch and Half Inch

Linear Measurement: Estimate, then measure to determine lengths. Determine how much longer one object is than another.

in. inch in. inch in. inch in. inch in. inch in. inch in. inch in. inch

© 2011 dma

estimate _____ **in.**   measurement _____ **in.**

estimate _____ **in.**   measurement _____ **in.**

estimate _____ **in.**   measurement _____ **in.**

estimate _____ **in.**   measurement _____ **in.**

estimate _____ **in.**   measurement _____ **in.**

estimate _____ **in.**   measurement _____ **in.**

Estimate, measure, record. Draw an equivalent line under each tab. Name an object or objects for each length.

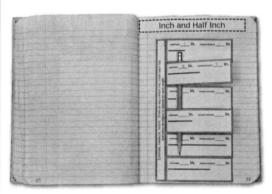

Inches and Centimeters

estimate _____ **in.**   measurement _____ **in.**

estimate _____ **cm**   measurement _____ **cm**

estimate _____ **cm**   measurement _____ **cm**

estimate _____ **cm**   measurement _____ **cm**

estimate _____ **in.**   measurement _____ **in.**

estimate _____ **cm**   measurement _____ **cm**

in. inch cm centimeter in. inch cm centimeter in. inch cm centimeter in. inch cm centimeter

© 2011 dma

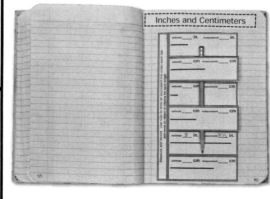

Inches and Centimeters

Measure and record. Use ruler to draw an
equivalent line under each tab and name an
object or objects for each length.

Linear Measurement: Estimate, then measure to determine lengths. Determine how much longer one object is than another.

in. inch in. inch in. inch in. inch in. inch in. inch in. inch in. inch in. inch

©2011 dma

estimate _____ in.   measurement _____ in.

estimate _____ in.   measurement _____ in.

estimate _____ in.   measurement _____ in.

estimate _____ in.   measurement _____ in.

estimate _____ in.   measurement _____ in.

estimate _____ in.   measurement _____ in.

Measure and record. Use ruler to draw an equivalent line under each tab. Name an object or objects for each length.

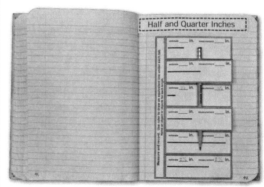

Convert Large to Small

Write equations under the tabs.

© 2011 dma

2 feet equal _____ inches.

1 yard equals _____ inches.

3 yards equal _____ feet.

4 yards equal _____ inches.

9 feet equal _____ yards.

1 mile equals _____ feet.

2 miles equal _____ feet.

1 mile equals _____ yards.

Write equations under the tabs.

© 2011 dma

1 meter equals _____ cm.

1 centimeter equals _____ mm.

1 kilometer equals _____ meters.

3 meters equal _____ cm.

2 centimeters equal _____ mm.

4 kilometers equal _____ meters.

8 centimeters equal _____ mm.

4 kilometers equal _____ meters.

Linear Measurement: Convert among different sized standard measurement units within a given measurement system.

© 2011 dma

120 inches
equal _____
feet.

36 inches
equal _____
feet.

48 inches
equal _____
feet.

24 inches
equal _____
feet.

© 2011 dma

5280 feet
equal _____
yards.

108 feet
equal _____
yards.

36 feet
equal _____
yards.

9 feet
equal _____
yards.

Title:

24

Convert Small to Large

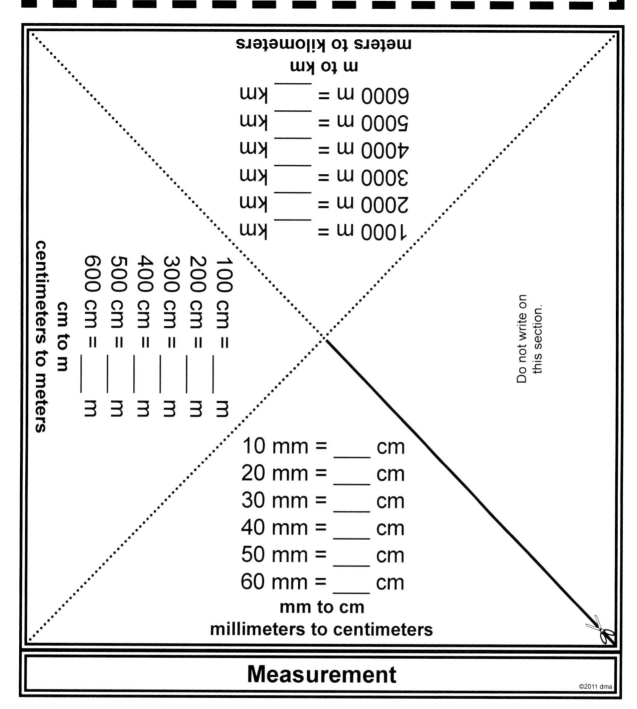

meters to kilometers

m to km

1000 m = ____ km
2000 m = ____ km
3000 m = ____ km
4000 m = ____ km
5000 m = ____ km
6000 m = ____ km

Do not write on this section.

centimeters to meters
cm to m

100 cm = ____ m
200 cm = ____ m
300 cm = ____ m
400 cm = ____ m
500 cm = ____ m
600 cm = ____ m

10 mm = ____ cm
20 mm = ____ cm
30 mm = ____ cm
40 mm = ____ cm
50 mm = ____ cm
60 mm = ____ cm

mm to cm
millimeters to centimeters

Measurement

©2011 dma

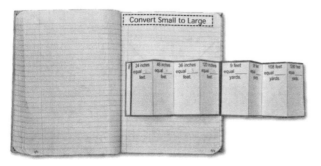

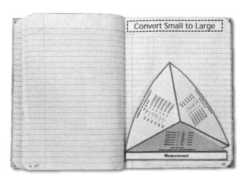

Convert Between Systems

Write equations under the tabs.

36 inches equal _____ centimeters.

10 feet equal _____ centimeters.

9 centimeters equal _____ inches.

500 millimeters equal _____ feet.

20 feet equal _____ meters.

156 inches equal _____ meters.

30 meters equal _____ inches.

5,000 kilometers equal _____ miles.

Write equations under the tabs.

12 yards equal _____ meters.

5 miles equal _____ meters.

66 meters equal _____ feet.

124 centimeters equal _____ inches.

2,640 feet equal _____ kilometers.

24 inches equal _____ millimeters.

91 meters equal _____ yards.

1000 millimeters equal _____ inches.

Linear Measurement: Convert among different sized standard measurement units within different measurement systems.

Washington Monument

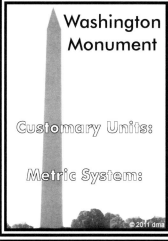

Customary Units:

Metric System:

Distance between Los Angeles and New York City

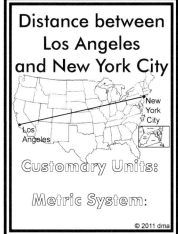

Customary Units:

Metric System:

Statue of Liberty

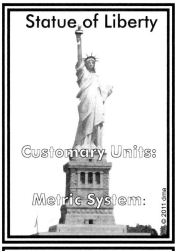

Customary Units:

Metric System:

Height of a Kodiak Bear

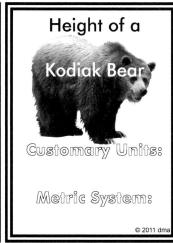

Customary Units:

Metric System:

Length of a Marker

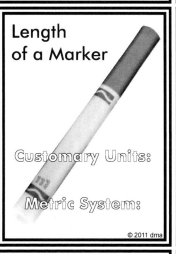

Customary Units:

Metric System:

Quarter

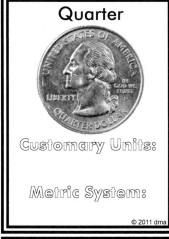

Customary Units:

Metric System:

Antarctica

Customary Units:

Metric System:

Length of a Pencil

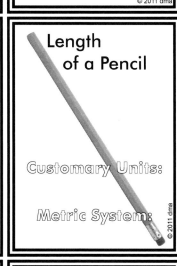

Customary Units:

Metric System:

Jefferson Memorial

Customary Units:

Metric System:

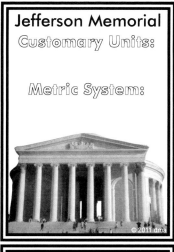

Length of a Ladybug

Customary Units:

Metric System:

Sport Utility Vehicle

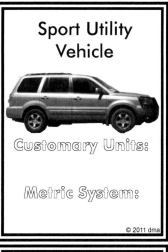

Customary Units:

Metric System:

Elevation of the Continental Divide

Customary Units:

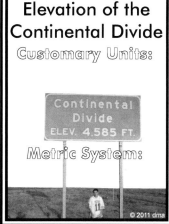

Continental Divide
ELEV. 4,585 FT.

Metric System:

Diameter of the Sun

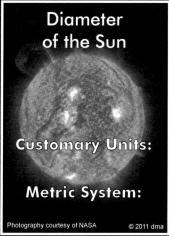

Customary Units:

Metric System:

Photography courtesy of NASA

Diameter of the Earth

Customary Units:

Metric System:

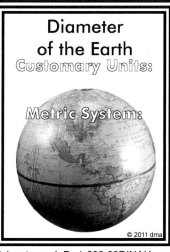

Nile River

Customary Units:

Metric System:

The White House

Customary Units:

Metric System:

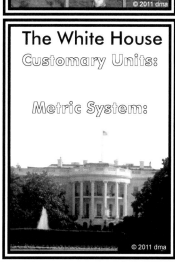

27

Word Problems

Word Problems

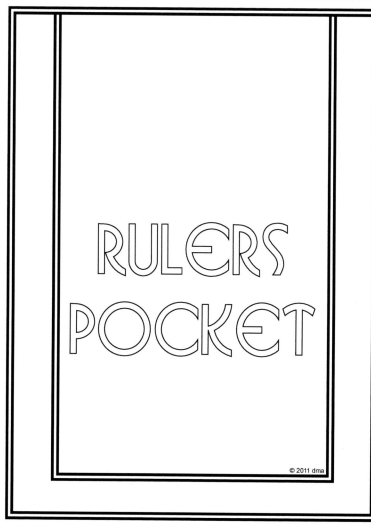

RULERS POCKET

length • width • length •

width • length • width • length •

A WORLD OF MEASUREMENTS POCKET

length • width • length

Rulers

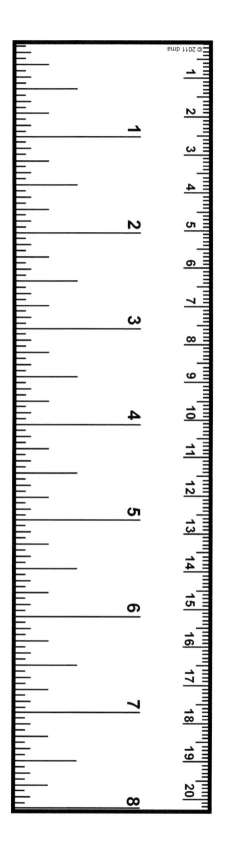
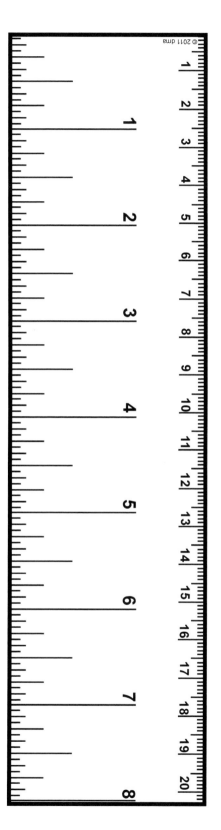

	When you want to convert:	To:	Multiply By:
Length:	inches centimeters yards meters miles kilometers	centimeters inches meters yards kilometers miles	2.54 0.39 0.91 1.09 1.61 0.62
Area:	cubic inches square centimeters square yards square meters square miles square kilometers	square centimeters square inches square meters square yards square kilometers square miles	16.39 0.16 0.83 1.19 2.59 0.39

© 2011 dma

Customary Length

12 inches = 1 foot
3 feet = 1 yard
5,280 feet = 1 mile
1,760 yards = 1 mile

Metric Length

10 millimeters = 1 centimeter
1000 millimeters = 1 meter
100 centimeters = 1 meter
1000 meters = 1 kilometer

Power Prefixes (Metric Unit Conversion)

mega-	M	1,000,000
kilo-	k	1,000
hecto-	h	100
deka-	da	10
uni-	-	1
deci-	d	0.1
centi-	c	0.01
milli-	m	0.001

* CCC113 $24.95

Notebook Foldables®
For Spirals, Binders, & Composition Books
Strategies for all Subjects 4th-College

Dinah's acclaimed book features adaptations of her Foldables® specially designed to fit in composition books, spiral notebooks, binders, and even exam books. Notebook Foldables® work well in any subject area to stimulate ideas and represent information in a format more familiar and useful to advanced/upper level students. Reproducible Notebook Foldable templates are supplied in the book, as well as instructions on how to create these modified Foldables using regular paper. This 129-page book contains over 400 full-color photos of examples of Notebook Foldables!

Includes CD!

Template from book

Example from book

Dual Winners of Teachers' Choice Awards!

Featured in *Learning* magazine (Jan. 2011)

Template from book

Example from book

Foldables®, Notebook Foldables®, & VKVs® for Spelling & Vocabulary
4th - 12th

This comprehensive 432-page photographic reference book contains over 1,600 color photos of Foldables®, Notebook Foldables®, and VKVs® (Visual Kinesthetic Vocabulary). It is organized alphabetically with sections including acronyms, analogies, antonyms, root words, synonyms, and more, with extensive word lists in each section. Spelling rules are noted in red within the word lists and throughout the book. Special word lists are presented in Venn diagram format to graphically illustrate relationships between sounds and different spellings. Includes Foldables, instructions, and VKV folding instructions! An amazing resource.

* CCC114 $49.95

Foldables® and VKVs® for Phonics, Spelling, and Vocabulary
PreK - 3rd

Dinah has compiled phonics, vocabulary, and spelling Foldables®, as well as word lists and Visual Kinesthetic Vocabulary® (VKV) flashcards, into this 350-page illustrated teaching manual with over 1,000 full-color photographs. The book is arranged in alphabetical order to enable quick searches of activities and word lists for teaching consonants, vowels, antonyms, synonyms, homographs, homophones, prefixes, suffixes, and more!

CCC112 $34.95